Rated "R"

Rated "R"

SHORT STORIES

Randy L. Townes

To order additional copies of this book, contact:
Xlibris Corporation
1-888-795-4274
www.Xlibris.com
Orders@Xlibris.com
64124

Chapter 1

As I am hypnotized by the smell of her perfume I draw her closer to me. If only she knew how I crave her body and how she has stricken me to my own insanity by wanting her soft touch. Her lips sing to me as I imagine my lips caressing hers as she shares the most tantalizing kiss. Her beauty is a mere painting of heaven itself which is the star of my art collection. The touch of her soft skin sends a tingle through my body breaking me down dragging me even further into bliss. My hands run down her back feeling the shape of her ass stimulating me as she smiles and giggles. She can feel the imprint of what is yet to be released against her leg as she licks her lips and moans letting me know she wants more. She walks to the bedroom shedding clothes with every step she takes. I watch closely never looking away while I throw my clothes across the room. She lays on the bed naked calling me closer every second I'm away. My penis rises as I watch her spread her legs and stroke her clit in circles making her river flow with wet. I walk closer to her biting my lip trying to keep my urge to go wild at bay. Her body touches mine as she sits up and grabs my penis in her hand and licks her lips and wraps them around my steel rod sucking it slowly moving back and forth. My hands graze her succulent nipples circling them over and over. She falls back on the bed and I climb on top of her kissing her neck moving downward letting my tongue taste the sweetness of her nipples. She moans when my lips kiss her curves and move toward her vortex of pleasure anticipating my tongue around her clit. I spread her lips apart and slowly suck and lick every inch of her with her wet dripping down my chin. I rise with my manhood standing at full attention dangling in the air ready to explore her tunnel of love. She gasps as she feels the full effect of it as it widens her lips and expands her walls. The sound of R. Kelly's 'Down Low' plays in the background as I grind and thrust in between her legs digging deeper and deeper. Her moans grow louder echoing through the walls as I move my hips in ways she can't imagine. She locks her legs around me holding on to that sweet satisfying feeling. The position killed me I had to switch. I got up and let the sweat roll off of my body as I told her to bend over. She grabbed the pillow and dug her face into it as I went deeper than before. The vibrations from her ass looked like tidal waves bouncing off of my hips. My hands rubbed down her back feeling there way to her nipples where I played with them to increase the satisfaction. She screamed, "Baby I'm about to come!" All I could do was go harder trying to reach my climax point before she reached hers. Sounds of love making echoed through the walls as her come ran down her leg. I stopped as she leaned over on the bed lying there silently with the silo wet of her naked body glowing from the candles. Her face expressions said it all as she felt at ease relaxed and satisfied.

Chapter 2

As she lies there asleep I can't help but think how lucky I am. The moon shines through the window hitting her at the right moment making her glow in the darkest of night. Her body calls to me wanting my touch or is it that I am under her spell. I pull the covers back and watch her sexy body laced in bra and panties dream of sweet dreams. Just looking at her made me erect. I unsnapped her bra and pulled it off, my tongue hung out of my mouth ready to lick her silk skin body. I moved down wrapping her panty line around my thumbs and started sliding them off her legs. I rubbed my face against her chest while my tongue licked and sucked on her nipples blowing on them making them hard with every gust of wind. Sweet moans flow from her soft lips as she bites them. I kiss on down letting my lips hit every soft spot on her body. She opens her legs for me as to say it needs me. I throw her legs over my shoulders and lay between her thighs. Her pussy was dripping wet and her clit stuck out begging for attention. I pressed my lips against her clit teasing her from my every touch tossing it around in my mouth like a piece of candy. My tongue dug into her ocean of seduction moving like waves crashing against the shore. She moaned louder rubbing her nipples as I was trying to suffocate myself in between her legs. She loosened her grip around my neck and called me to her. Yea baby, I said eagerly wanting her? Give it to me, she replied. She grabbed my boxers and slid them off staring at my penis amazed at my size. It made me laugh when she would over exaggerate. She grabbed it and slid it in. I started slow at first then she moaned faster. I put my arms under her legs bending them back toward her chest and then went faster. The sound of slapping skin echoed through the room as I hit harder and harder trying to deliver to her expectations. She turned to her side and crossed her leg sticking her ass in the air; I stuck my penis in once again. Her pussy felt warm against my skin as I grinded my hips into her ass twirling my penis around inside her vagina. She screamed, "Baby keep going! The sweat rolled off of my face and dripped on to my chest. Her nails gripped the sheets as she stuffed the pillow in her mouth biting it from the amazing feeling. She rubbed on her nipples as I grinded deeper. She moaned, "Do you like it baby?" I had to say yes as her sweet bliss took control over me. "I'm coming baby, she replied." I went faster speeding up the climax her leg started to shake and then she screamed louder than ever before, once her come ran down her leg I knew she had came. I had to pull out as I was close and then it happened; I pulled out and my come shot out like a rocket landing on her beautiful ass, sweet satisfaction.

Chapter 3

I walked in the door and to my surprise I see her there naked on the couch. She looked at me as I looked at her not saying a word. I asked her what she was doing. She looked at me with her hypnotizing eyes and her sexy lips and said I want you to play with it. She spread her legs and like a moth to a light I walked toward her. I gave her a kiss and then I laid back on the couch as she laid between my legs. She grabbed my hands and placed one on her breast and ran the other one down her body moaning as she got closer to her cave of seduction. I grew harder by the minute my steel rod fought to be free. She closed her eyes and laid back as my fingers ran in and out of her circling around her clit. I dug my fingers into her vagina stroking it slowly getting it wetter from every motion. I massaged her nipple making it hard every time I twirled my finger around it. She started moving her hips gyrating against my fingers as I could barely grip her clit from the wet. She moaned, "Oh baby as I took her mind to a fantasy world where all her dreams came true." My penis jumped constantly trying to escape the prison he was in. I stroked her clit around and around looking every second not wanting to miss a thing. She paused and told me to take off my clothes; I took them off as fast as I could releasing the beast from his cage. I laid back down on the couch and she walked to me looking sexier than ever, breast bouncing in the air from every step she took. She proceeded to climb on top of me and then she swung her leg over my face knowing I had a taste for candy as she wrapped her lips around my penis. Her ass was so round and beautiful I couldn't keep my hands off of it. Her clit hung from her vagina calling me to come lick it. She stroked my penis up and down while she licked and sucked it like a lollipop. I slid my fingers in her wet valley going in and out while my lips locked on her clit as my tongue drove her crazy. She gripped the pillows trying to bare the excitement my tongue gave her. She was close as was I almost reaching that climax point. She screamed with pleasure as her come flowed from her vagina and dripped down my tongue. She kept beating my penis massaging my head with her tongue. "I'm coming baby, I exclaimed!" As my eyes rolled in the back of my head I erupted. She kept sucking until the come dripped from her chin. We both rose from the couch took a shower and smiled as to what just happened played back in our heads.

Chapter 4

I could smell her fragrance in the air intensifying my urge drawing me closer to her. I walked upstairs and opened the door and there she stood dripping wet. The steam rushed by my face and then cleared leaving the image of her naked body relaxing in the shower. I slid back the door and there she was letting the soap run down her back still bathing as if I weren't watching. She looked at me and smiled and gave me a look hinting me to join her. I took off my shirt as she stood by the shower door watching me, touching herself rubbing her nipples teasing me even more. My pants hit the floor and she smiled inviting me into her domain. The water hit my shoulders and she watched it race down my body as to see who would be the winner. She grabbed the soap and walked toward me rubbing me down as I stood there. As we switched places and she stepped toward the shower head I watched her. I watched the water run down her body and curve around her vagina as she opened her legs and there I stood penis rising by the minute licking my lips as I wanted a taste wanting to drink the water as it ran from her breast. I stepped toward her kissing her neck from behind with my penis pressing against her ass letting her know I wanted more. "Baby," she moaned? "Shhh," I replied. I turned her around and fell to my knees as I propped one of her legs around my shoulders and began kissing her clit as the water showered over my head. She grabbed the shower head with one hand and held on as she took the other and began pushing my head in deeper. I wanted to go deeper as if I was trying to see how long I could hold my breath under water. My fingers ran in and out of her as my chin dripped with wet from her pool of pleasure. I stood and took both of her legs and wrapped them around me as I held her in my arms. She grabbed my penis and slid it in. I went slow taking precaution because of the wet floor. I pressed her against the shower door getting my balance then stroking her, grinding between her legs watching my million dollar man move in and out as her moans echoed through the bathroom walls. She kept moaning breathing heavier than before. Her vagina felt like sweet bliss as she moved her hips along with mine. My tongue twirled around her fat nipples as if I were licking ice cream sucking on them increasing her stimulation. I stopped and she climbed down and stepped toward the shower head and bent over. "Come on baby give it to me," she said. My hands gripped her ass filling the roundness and the firmness of it. I slid him in going in deeper from the position we were in, she threw her head back as she felt the full effect of my penis. The water ran down her back dripping from her ass. She screamed, "Go faster baby moaning from pleasure and pain." I can't explain the feeling of watching her round ass coming back on my hips. The water flowed from her vagina as to think it was dripping wet and every time I hit it hard her breast would bounce back and forth as she held them, circling her nipples around and around. I stroked faster and faster holding on to the shower door to keep my balance. She spread her legs and bent over even more propping her ass in the air letting me hit it harder. She moaned, "I'm coming baby." She stroked her clit as I grinded repeatedly and then she screamed, she cried out with pleasure. "I'm coming baby," I muttered. "I want you to come on me," she said. I kept going then I pulled out and watched my come shoot out of my penis and on to her back and as she stood she smiled at me reassuring me that I was her black Adonis.

Chapter 5

Sleepless nights tormented me as I laid there awake staring at the ceiling thinking of ways to get to sleep. I looked over and there she was sound asleep with a look on her face like nothing could bother her. I eased out of bed and went down stairs to the kitchen. I cut on the light and looked in the fridge trying not to make to much noise. To my surprise I could hear her coming down the stairs so I waited by the door because I knew she would be walking through at any second. The door swung open and there was the image of a goddess laced in bra and panties. She asked me what I was doing. So I had to tell her the long story of how I couldn't get to sleep and figured I would get a late night snack. She walked over to me with a sexy look on her face and said a snack huh. I smiled at the thoughts that were running through my head. She walked to the refrigerator and bent over toward my way showcasing her ass as the main dish. She looked back at me teasing me giggling to herself as she knew she already had me hypnotized by her hips. I could feel the blood rushing to my head making me erect as I watched her. She walked over to the table ass switching and jiggling as her cheeks hung out of her panties. She hopped on the table and laid back and threw the chocolate syrup and whipped cream at me and told me to eat her. She laid on the table while I walked around her circling her as if she were my patient. My hands ran down her silky smooth body touching every curve she had. I unsnapped her bra and revealed her beautiful full breasts with her nipples steady getting hard as I twirled my fingers around her areola. My hands slid down her sides catching her panty line within my grip. I pulled them off slowly not wanting to miss a second of her sweet essence being showcased as the main course. I grabbed the chocolate and poured some on her nipples letting it run a little then taking my tongue and licking it up until I got to her nipples which I sucked and licked repeatedly. "Baby you are making it worse," she exclaimed! How I asked then I asked her did she want me to lick it and she nodded. I climbed on the table in between her legs and laid between her thighs. Her clit stuck out calling to me feigning for my lips, my touch, and the way I moved it around with my tongue. She moaned and moved her hips in circles as I dug deeper into her candy with my tongue. Her vagina dripped with wet and my chin was covered in it. I stood on my knees taking my boxers off before my penis ripped through them. I took him out and rubbed her clit with it making her want it even more then she said, "Baby give it to me." I spread her lips apart and ease my penis in. The warmth and tightness of it felt amazing I could only compare it to a butterfly in his cocoon. I positioned my arms underneath her legs bending them back toward her chest and started hitting hard. The kitchen table squeaked and moved as we were going at it, magazines dropped to the floor from all the vibrations. I liked to watch my penis go in and out of her watching the wetness pour out of her as I went harder. She took my head and shoved into her breasts lips kissing them, tongue licking her nipples going faster and faster. I loosened my grip and she locked her legs around my back making sure I wasn't going anywhere. She screamed, "Harder baby harder!" So I went harder until you could only hear the sound of her screaming and the sound of my skin slapping against hers. She moaned, "I'm coming baby." She drew me close to her as I kept stroking, grinding harder and then she screamed letting out a roar of pleasure running her nails down my back trying to control her orgasm. Even though she had just came she was still grinding with me moving her hips along with mine helping me reach my climax. I looked at her nipples bouncing back and forth then looked at her sweet vagina then ran my hands around to her ass and then it happened I pulled out of her and shot like a cannon watching it land on her stomach. Sweet climax nothing ever felt better. I leaned in for a kiss then eased off the table holding the star of the show in my hands. Are you going to sleep now, she asked? I smiled at her and said, "Yes thank you baby."

Chapter 6

She sat beside me smiling looking beautiful. I stared at her lips as she talked wanting to kiss them. I laid her on the bed as I climbed on top of her kissing those soft lips and moving my hands down her sides feeling her smooth skin. I stood to take my shirt off letting her feel my chest and my abs as I showcased them for her. I looked at her as she looked at me with a look of desire. She threw her hands above her head as I slid her shirt off. I started kissing her neck, hypnotized from her body I kept going down. She unbuckled her belt and took her pants off unveiling her sexy ass as it made its appearance. My eyes watched her as if they were scopes and I had a missile that was looking for a target. She smiled at me because I couldn't take my eyes off of her. Her body called for me called for my lips to kiss her. I kissed lower around her belly button and on down and as I drew closer to her seductive candy she got wetter. I grabbed her soaking wet panties with my teeth and pulled them off. She closed her legs shy to the fact that it was her first time letting me down there, I laughed though. I ran my fingers down her thighs rubbing down one and kissing up the other spreading her legs apart as her clit feigned for my tongue. As she opened her legs I could only think what a beautiful site as her vagina dripped with wet. I teased her a little kissing everything except what she wanted me to. She pulled her lips back and her fat clit stuck out calling to me as it needed the most attention. My lips kissed her clit gently sucking on it as I went deeper with my tongue, her moans grew louder. My tongue slid smoothly across her clit as I tossed it around doing things to her with my tongue even I couldn't believe. I put her legs on my shoulders as if I were wearing her vagina like a face mask. My hands circled around her nipples intensifying what magic I was creating. My penis hurt like hell as it was locked away but I knew he would be released soon. I kept licking faster then slowly trying to control my tongue as she ran her fingers through my hair pushing my head in deeper. Her moans became constant growing louder as she moved her hips. She screamed, "I'm coming baby; my only reply was that I kept licking!" It felt like time stood still as she arched her back and moaned with excitement. I stood up and she slid to the edge of the bed grabbing my pants pulling them down. I stepped out of them and there I stood naked in front of her. She grabbed my penis and kissed the tip of it and then she used her tongue to lick around it. I laid her back on the bed and climbed on top of her. I grabbed my penis and slid it in slowly. She gasped as it widened her vagina every inch it went in. The feeling of warm wet bliss felt amazing. I started stroking moving my hips as she spread her legs even further letting me go deeper. She wrapped her arms around my back holding me close to her as I thrusted and grinded against her vagina. My name echoed through the room as it flowed from her lips like a soft melody. She moaned in my ear as I moaned in hers telling her that it was good and that it was just what I needed. A few minutes went by and she rolled me over and climbed on top of me kissing my chest and rubbing me down with her hands. My hands gripped her ass as if I were holding on to dear life. She started moving her hips throwing my penis around inside of her vagina. Her skin felt like silk when I ran my hands down her body. She went faster; "I moaned I'm coming baby." She leaned toward me as I held her, my hips pounding against hers and then it happened I blew like a volcano. She kept grinding for a minute then stopped and fell back in my arms.

Chapter 7

We walked hand in hand down on the beach watching the tide come in closer and closer as we ran away to keep our feet from getting wet. She stopped and looked out at the ocean and told me to watch it with her. I walked up behind her and put my arms around her holding her tantalizing body. We stood there watching the sunset and then I leaned in and kissed her on the neck. She smiled and told me I should stop before something happens. Of course I didn't listen so I kissed her neck again. She turned around and started kissing me. My hands ran down her back gripping her ass squeezing it firmly. She looked at me and in a soft voice she said, "Its wet baby." I smiled and looked around and then I started kissing her. As the night grew closer she laid down on the beach calling me down to her. I climbed on top of her kissing her rolling around in the sand my hands running down her every curve. As night appeared and the moon glowed in the sky she took her clothes off as I did the same. A chill ran through the wind but I kept her body warm with mine. I kissed her neck and her round nipples licking them twirling my tongue around them. My fingers stroked her clit and ran in and out of her. Her lake of desire got getting wetter and wetter while my penis rose getting harder. She moaned, "Stick it in baby." I reached in my pants and pulled him out sliding it in stroking slowly with the sound of crashing water in the background as the water smashed against the rocks. She locked her legs around my back not letting go as she wanted more. Our hands ran down each others body massaging one another. Her hands wrapped around my hips as she started pulling me in going deeper and harder and faster. I stopped for a second then told her to bend over. I got behind her looking at her ass as she stood it up and eased it in rubbing my hands across her thick ass as it glowed from the moonlight. I gripped her hips and started going faster pounding harder. She cried out, "Keep going baby don't stop." Her breast bounced back and forth from the vibrations rippling through her body. Her hands dug in the sand as I kept hitting her spot getting her closer to her climax. I placed my hands on her shoulders pulling her back toward me going deeper as she propped her ass in the air begging for me to smack it. The moon shined on her ass making it look like a peach coming back on my hips. She screamed, "I'm close baby!" I kept beating her vagina listening to the sounds of slapping skin echo through the air. Just when I thought things couldn't get any better she erupted like a volcano letting out a tremendous scream. I kept going for a few seconds then stopped. I pulled out and fell back on the beach; she fell over letting the wind cool her down as the sound of the ocean took her away.

Chapter 8

She walked in the room wearing only a towel and my eyes locked on to her. She had just come out of the shower dripping wet and all I wanted to do was lick her dry. Suddenly this urge came over me, no more like a trance when I watched her lotion her legs. She stood up and started walking out the door and then that's when I saw my chance. I got up and raced to her and forced her against the wall kissing her my hands rubbing on her ass gripping it getting a hand full. She threw her arms around my head surprised at the fact that I was really getting into it. I stripped the towel off and ran my fingers in between her legs stroking her clit while I kissed her nipples sucking on them like gumdrops. Her moans only drove me further to satisfy. She stood against the wall as I groped and kissed her all over. I went lower and fell to my knees as I got the urge to go for a swim in her lake of ecstasy. I pulled my fingers out of her sweet candy and threw her leg over my shoulder as I was about to taste the sweetness of her clit. I spread her lips apart and wrapped my tongue around it. She couldn't believe what was happening to her; she closed her eyes and forced my head in deeper. Her moans filled the air along with the sound of me licking and slurping up her juices. I twirled my tongue all around not missing a spot. While my tongue occupied her clit my fingers ran in going deeper inside of her. I stood up and dropped my pants releasing the monster which dangled in the air hard as a rock. I picked her up and held her against the wall as she locked her legs around my back. I slid it in with ease from all the wet that was pouring out of her vagina. She screamed, "Oh baby as she began to come down on my penis faster and harder." She held me close to her, her breathing grew heavier as I went deeper pounding her ass against the wall while I kept my balance. Her lips felt so soft and her tongue rolled around mine like a snake. She got aroused when she ran her hands down my body feeling the muscles as they stood out from me holding her. This felt so good her body against mine creating friction in the moment. She moaned, "Keep going baby I'm about to!" I kept going giving her all I had as I was coming close to my erupting point. I dug my feet into the ground and went faster pounding harder sending vibrations through her ass listening to the sounds of her sweet voice echoing through the walls trying to make her come. She screamed out, "Baby!" She clutched me within her arms and held me close screaming my name as she climaxed. Her come dripped from my shaft as it made it wetter sending a tingle through the tip of my penis and then it happened I climaxed. She kissed me as we fell to the floor still on one another still grinding against me until there was nothing left.

Chapter 9

We sat in the car talking in a mall parking lot watching security drive back and forth. Even with only a little light shining upon her face she glowed with radiance, every time she spoke I watched her sweet lips move wanting to kiss them fighting the urge to kiss her. She could be mine if only. The only thing in my way from kissing her like I wanted to was my armrest which divided us. I pushed it back grabbed a cd and hit play and as the slow music beat from my speakers I drew closer to her. She could tell what was about to happen as her eyes sparkled while she looked at me. As I inched closer I could smell her; sweet. She braced herself as our lips connected. I reclined the seats taking her down, she threw her arms around me as my hands found there way in between her legs. I went under her shirt the softest skin I've ever felt her belly was so smooth my fingers ran down past her belly ring. She went under me as I was so close that I could've been on top and unbuckled my belt, one step closer. She whispered to me, "Baby you have gotten me so wet." I stopped for a second and drew my attention to her pants and proceeded to unzip them. I slid them down just a little only to show what I needed. As I pulled them off I could feel the warmth coming from her vagina. I looked at her as I started at her panty line and went under getting closer to her clit and there it was as she gasped when my fingers slid down. I laid back down next to her kissing her soft lips, kissing her neck, taking my other hand and going up her shirt playing with her nipples as I stroked her clit with my fingers. I had enough I couldn't take it anymore I pulled her shirt up and pulled down her bra revealing her creamy breast, nipples ready to be licked. I leaned in as my tongue stuck out licking across her nipples lips kissing them sucking them gently. Her moans were almost as loud as the music playing. My fingers slid from left to right trying to get some friction so I could stroke her clit like I wanted to. I went deeper inside of her pleasuring her as my hand took control over her vagina. She grabbed my head and kissed me as I went faster spreading her legs as far as the door would let her. "Keep going baby," she moaned. I loved the feeling of her juicy clit in between my grip stroking it, massaging it, teasing it, oh how bad I wanted to have her clit in my mouth bouncing it around with my tongue. She grabbed me moaning louder gripping the seats and then she paused. Her vagina flooded with come and my fingers were drowning. "Oh baby," she sounded relaxed, at ease. I pulled my hand out and wiped it off with a towel I had in the back seat and sat back up. She came to after a couple of seconds and looked at me and smiled. She leaned over and gave me a kiss placing her hand directly on my penis. "Damn baby," she exclaimed! What, "I answered back?" She put her hands down my pants and pulled him out hard as hell standing at full attention. She leaned down and stuck out her tongue licking down my shaft coming back up wrapping her lips around my head. I gripped the steering wheel looking around the parking lot for anybody passing through. Her tongue felt amazing. She licked my head like ice cream.

She went down then up, damn I couldn't control it she had my eyes rolling in the back of my head. Her silky tongue sent a tingle through my body. She sat up beating my penis and then I came. I shot like a rocket from all this built up tension from what I wanted to do to her. She grabbed the towel and cleaned herself up. She kissed me and got out of the car and into hers and said goodbye and left, until next time baby.

Chapter 10

She walks in the room smiling at me as I am laid across the bed watching TV. She jumped on the bed laughing trying to be funny shaking me up. She falls on top of me and lies on my chest running her hands against my skin. She lifts her head and starts kissing me. I dropped the remote on the floor and place my hands on her ass letting her know I want more. My hands go under her pants and find there way to her fat ass and then her button popped off, she didn't care though. She stood up and cut the TV off and turned the radio on and positioned herself in the middle of the floor getting ready for her début. I stood up and locked eyes on to her watching her shake her ass swaying and moving her hips. She danced for me moving so swift so slowly it was amazing. My penis stood straight up as I took him out ready for that wet candy to slide down on it. She moved like fire dancing and moving in everyway. She lifted up her shirt and threw it aside moving her hips from side to side as she pushed her pants down while she moved. She walked toward me slowly showing off her body trying to see how bad I wanted it and I wanted it bad.

Her attempt to tease me only drove me crazy I had to have her body in my hands her nipple against my lips and her clit against my tongue. I stood up and grabbed her and held her close kissing her on to the bed climbing on top of her taking control kissing her neck rubbing my hands down her body teasing her myself only as payback. I unsnapped her bra and threw it on the floor then pulled her panties off and did the same not wasting any time to satisfy her. As I kissed her body I asked her; "What do you want me to do to you?" She could barely answer me from all the moaning and gasping she was doing. She whispered to me, "Baby everything is yours." Those were the words that I wanted to here. I told her to sit up on her knees and then I slid under her letting her grind on my face as her clit rubbed against my tongue. She moved her hips in circles then stroked back and forth on my face. Slowly she moved as I sucked on her clit licking it trying to catch it in my mouth so I could tease it. She held her position while I ran my hands across her ass gripping it going further putting my fingers in her vagina as she rode them. She moaned and screamed as the feeling was too good to handle. She stopped and then slid down to my rod of steel and slid it in saying, "I want it baby." While the music played she grinded against me creating friction stimulating the feeling I was getting. My hands couldn't hold on as she was moving her hips in so many ways. I finally grabbed her ass and dug my hips into her vagina hitting hard as she leaned on me holding me taking all of this in. She cried out digging her nails into my back as she came down repeatedly on my penis getting her vagina wetter. I slowed down and licked her breast circling her nipples with my tongue and then that's when she felt it she screamed, "Baby keep going!" I stopped licking and began to beat it up pounding her ass she screamed, "Faster so I went faster she screamed harder so I hit harder while the sweat rolled down my body." She grabbed the sheets and held them as I hit her spot making her come watching it drip from her vagina down my penis making it wet and moist. Damn . . .

Chapter 11

The sun comes through the window shinning through the curtains giving the room a burning glow of red. She knocks at the door and before I open it I try to imagine what she is wearing. Our eyes connect and she smiles as I invite her in. she walks in and looks around complementing on my furniture and my choice of colors. I give her a tour of my house, she walks through the house getting more comfortable with her surroundings and she sees the door, my door. "What's in there," she asked? I grab her by the hand and guide her into the room. She walks into the fiery red room smiling liking how the room filled with color as the sun shined through the curtains. I closed the door and walked toward her showing off my electronics which I was proud of. She sat on the bed looking around and then she saw my stereo and decided to cut it on. I turned around and there she was dancing. I sat back and watched her as her hips swayed from side to side. I got up and walked behind her, I startled her for a second but she kept dancing. I placed my hands on her hips moving with her as she danced to the beat. My eyes watched her round ass move as thoughts ran through my head about how her jeans hugged her every curve, she was beautiful. I pulled her close to me pressing her ass against my hips holding her in my arms as she threw her head back on my chest. The sweet smell of her body spray filled the room driving me even crazier wanting her, feigning for her. I could tell she enjoyed my company, my warmth as I held her. She turned around and threw her arms around me pressing her breast against my chest. I brushed her hair back and leaned in closely to her neck and kissed her. She clutched my shirt within her hands moaning softly. I kissed her again licking slowly, gently up and down her neck. She kept moaning kissing my neck wanting it to go further, she went under my shirt rubbing down my back feeling the cuts in my body from my muscles. I tilted her head back and kissed her, her lips felt like clouds pressed against mine. Her mouth opened wider letting her tongue slither from hers to mine twirling around mine sliding against on another. I slid my hands down her back around her ass grasping it bringing it closer to me. I drew back still kissing her lips and I began to unbuckle her belt and unzip her pants. She did the same taking it off and throwing it on the floor. She rubbed down my abs underneath the brim of my boxers and grabbed the heavy hitter and as she held it in her hand she let out a seductive moan. I picked her up and placed her on the bed kissing and rubbing her every curve. I stood to take off my shirt and pants showing the big bulge I had in my boxers. I climbed on top of her and unbuttoned her shirt one by one. She looked at me watching me undress her as she brushed against my penis wanting it. I grabbed the edges of her pants and pulled them off. She sat up and unsnapped her bra looking at me as I stood there light reflecting off of my body glowing from the shades of red. I slid my boxers off letting my manhood hang free as he was the main attraction and my tongue was the host of this sex show. She stared at it biting her lip wanting it inside of her vagina. I slid her to the edge of the bed and grabbed her panties and slid them past her feet. She opened her legs and there was the prize winner. Her forbidden fruit poured with wet running down like water curving around her ass. Her clit stuck out like a hook and I was the catch of the day. I climbed on top of her kissing those soft lips again addicted to them. I kissed down smelling her body spray all over making me crave. My fingers circled around her hard nipples licking my lips as I slid it across them sucking on them playing with them. My tongue stuck out licking down her body stopping at the edge of her pleasurable secrets. I bent down lying between her legs throwing them over my shoulders isolating myself within her vagina. I kissed her clit, she moaned. I kissed it again she threw her head back from pleasure. I sucked her clit within my mouth and twirled it around licking it stroking it with my tongue. She moved her legs curling her toes trying to control the feeling. I slid my tongue across her clit inside of her vagina her lips covered my mouth as I dug my face into it. I stood and wiped the wet from my mouth and climbed in between her legs. I looked at her then at my penis and placed him at the gates of ecstasy. I took position and slid him in, she gasped and moaned feeling the full effect of it as it went in inch by inch. She placed her hands around my head locking her legs around my back ready for what's about to take place. I start grinding slowly loving the image of my penis covered in her wet stroking in between her legs. I moved my hips giving her more than what she asked for. As I moved my hands I massaged her breast as my fingers played with her nipples covering every area that I could satisfy. She was amazing everything about her drew me to her. Our bodies rubbed against each other as my chest was on top of hers holding her. She kissed me, kissed my neck her hands felt so soft moving down my body. I fell under her spell as she moaned in my ear using her tongue to lick my neck. I stroked faster our bodies inner twined she cried out as I hit her spot over and over again. "Keep going baby," she moaned! Her moans grew constant and as she held me tight she experienced a mind blowing orgasm. A tear fell from her eye and her come gushed from her vagina as I kept stroking. She held me close not letting go until I had came. She whispered, "Give it to me baby." My eyes rolled and my body tightened as I was about to release. I dug my face into the sheets and let things take there course. I paused for a second and took my hands and held hers trying to control the feeling while letting the come flow from my penis and as we came back to reality and I noticed me on top of her and the sound of Maxwell playing in the background; we connected. As I looked in her eyes I knew then it was something deeper than what it seemed to be.

Chapter 12

The rays from the sun pierce through the green leaves as we walk through the woods hiking to the creek I had in my backyard. It was a beautiful day I couldn't ask for anything better. She looked cute with her little hiking boots on even though I knew she hated the woods, she was brave though. She had her hair in pigtails despite the fact she knew I was crazy about pigtails and even crazier about her. We stopped for a second to take a brake; she dropped her bags gasping for air. I laughed because she was tired already and we've had only walked less than a mile. I grabbed her bags and kept going she followed shortly. When we arrived at the creek we unpacked and sat for a while. We talked and laughed and had a little time to sit back and look at the scenery, it was beautiful. I looked up and the clouds slowly changed from a puffy white to a cloudy gray. The sky rumbled and the rain slowly poured down from the skies. She screamed telling me to hurry but I didn't mind the rain. Suddenly it grew heavy and it was too late to try and beat the rain. She stood there sobbing and weeping, I thought it was funny but I knew I couldn't laugh. I walked over by the creek and stood beside her and brushed the wet hair back from her face. "It's okay sweetie," I said. She looked at me with that said face and shook her head as to say the world is over and all because of a little rain. I held her in my arms and gave her a kiss. I started to remove my hand and she grabbed me. She looked at me with a look I've never seen before a look of desire. She drew closer to me until our bodies connected. She leaned in and placed her lips upon mine. I couldn't explain what I felt from that kiss. I put my hands on her waist and pulled her close to me. I stepped back from her and let her take my wet shirt off as I took hers off. I leaned against a tree and watched her ease out of her pants enjoying the show before my eyes. She walked over to me rubbing my chest my abs as the water ran from my shoulders down my body. She unzipped my pants and pulled them to the ground along with my boxers. She stood and unsnapped her bra and slid her panties past her knees and off her feet. She walked over to me kissing me touching me in the right places in the right ways. Her tongue felt exhilarating against my skin. The rain fell from the trees on her body racing down her breast stopping at the tip of her nipple where it stayed until I licked it. I held her breast in my hand while I licked her nipples sucking on them circling them with my tongue as they grew hard from the cold rain. I laid her down on the ground on top of our clothes, rain still pouring on our naked bodies. I lay on top of her kissing her neck my penis sinking in like quick sand sliding in easy from her wet. Her eyes widened and her moans echoed through the woods as she felt it going in deeper than she thought. I rested my head on her breast still licking and sucking her soft nipples as I held them in my mouth biting them gently and kissing them softly. Her nails dug into my back as I kept stroking. Her screams almost sounded like cries but there were no tears. What we were doing wasn't just sex it was something deeper another level of passion that we shared with each other. She stared in my eyes as I stared in hers not looking away connecting with her inner soul. She pulled me down and kissed me and wrapped her arms around me. Her skin shined radiantly when the little light that shined through the leaves hit her. She whispered, "Wait." I answered back, "What is it?" She didn't say a word she just rolled me over and climbed on top of me. She arched her back and pulled her hair back as her hips swayed back forth. Her breast stood out sitting perfect on her chest as my hands held them and my thumbs twirled her nipples. I guided her hips back and forth looking at her vagina as it threw my penis around inside of it. She placed her hand on my chest keeping her balance as she grinded harder. The birds flew from the trees startled by her moans as they grew louder every time I hit her spot. She locked her legs under mine and laid on my chest wrapping her arms around me while I placed my hands on her thick ass and started stroking. Her nipples rubbed against mine as I bounced her up and down on my ride of love. Her entire body was wet which made it easy for her to slide up and down on it. The rain was cold but she kept me warm. She whispered, "Baby give it to me just like that." Her seductive moans drove me further to satisfy her. She rose up and began kissing me shoving her tongue down my mouth. She ran her fingers through my hair while stroking her body along with mine. She looked at me with those eyes burning holes through my heart and screamed, "I'm coming baby." I went faster trying to speed the climax. I watched as her eyes rolled in the back of her head, the come flowing from her river of ecstasy. I held on to her ass still stroking taking all she wanted to give. She dug her hands into the dirt trying to find something anything to hold on to. Her moans sounded so sweet so amazing. She caught her breath and laid back down on my chest as I wrapped my arms around her. As I looked up and watched the trees sway back and forth and the sun still shining I couldn't help but feel like nature itself watched us make love.

Chapter 13

Her breasts sit gracefully within my hands embracing her cocoa brown nipples with my silky tongue. She opens her legs enticing me with her essence, wet pouring like a waterfall isolated within the depths of a cave. The aroma of sweet pea fragrance rolls off of her body casting a spell upon my mind as I am stricken to be her sex slave. I kiss ever so gently down her belly resting my head at the gates of ecstasy. I lick my lips and place them on her clit making it disappear within my mouth sucking it and massaging it. She spreads her lips apart as to tell me where and what she wants licked. I kneel as she is my queen and let my tongue swim within her sweet dark abyss. She takes my head and pushes it in deeper begging for me to reach the middle, the epicenter of her chocolate fountain. Her eyes rolled in the back of her head as her moans sounded like sweet passion flowing from her soft lips. I moved my head all around not sticking to the movement of just my tongue I wanted to feel the full effect of having her lips curved around mine as I teased her clit. I stood and stepped back taking a second to myself trying to control what wanted to be unleashed. She walked over to me grasping my shirt within her hands pulling it over my head and throwing it on the floor. I tried to stand tall, stand straight but every time her lips touched my skin she broke me down. She knew just where to touch me, where to kiss me, where to lick me. Her hands rubbed down my body creeping beneath my boxers wanting to feel it in her hands. Her lips, the softest touch to a man ran down my body kissing my chest, the creases in my abs. She kneeled and unbuttoned my pants and pulled them down anxious to see what I had as he stood erect trying to see daylight. She pulled them down slowly until they hit the floor and pushed me on the bed with my missile at launch position ready for lift off. I couldn't believe this was happening. She walked over to me and kissed my stomach and on down, my penis jumped with excitement. She kissed my head and ran her tongue down my shaft torturing me as I wanted her to do more. She kissed the tip of my penis her lips spreading as she went down my rod of steel opening her mouth further and further. As I watched I came to a conclusion that as she sucked it seemed like this was competition and she was an all star. Her breast hung from her chest as she bent over, I reached out to them circling her nipples making her river run once again. I brushed the hair back from her face wanting to see her tongue at work exciting me by the minute. As I played with her nipples and watched her wipe away the wet running down her leg it was time. I stopped her and called her to me telling her to join me on the bed where her destiny awaited. She laid down on the bed as I stood to take position. I grabbed her legs and pulled her to me climbing on top of her kissing her as I was about to enter the gates of ecstasy. Melodies of soft moans echoed from her lips filling my head with songs of pleasure. The way her body responded to mine and the way we connected it was more of making love than sex. I took my time catering to her every need, her smooth skin, her breast, and her silky legs. She slid her legs around my back locking one around the other as I grinded against her wet vagina. The moonlight shined through the window reflecting off of her beautiful skin giving her a shade of blue eyes sparkling from the light as she looked at me. Every second of pleasure she expressed upon her face by giving me ooo's and ahhh's. She ran her hands down my tight body my muscles flexing from the constant grinding. I slid my hand down her leg curving around her thick ass grasping it as it sent tingles through my body. I dug deeper within her vagina wondering how far her tunnel of love will take me. My lips covered her chest with kisses kissing her breasts and nipples licking them as if they were mountains of ice cream topped of with Hershey kisses. She dug her nails in my back lashing out from the pleasure of my tongue around her nipples and my hips thrusting in between her legs. The mood struck once again she unlocked her legs from around me and pushed me off. I stood ready to deliver wondering what the hell she was doing. She rolled over on her knees coming back to the edge of the bed kneeling down making her ass blossom like a flower. I stepped forward taking control grabbing her thick rump within my hands squeezing it firmly. She ran her hands between her legs opening the gates again inviting me in. I grabbed her shoulders and pulled her back to me making it hard for her to escape my grip. I stroked my hand across her back feeling her ass every chance I could. She reached for the pillow and dug her face into it to keep her screams from waking the neighbors. I reached for her nipples playing with them as I kept a tight grip on her body. I didn't know which sound I loved more her moans or the sound of my penis slapping against her vagina. I grabbed her hips and threw them back against my waist going faster trying to deliver what I promised. She looked back and called out to me giving me signs that I was hitting the right places. She moaned with such beauty such passion. She grabbed my hand and held it while I kept stroking from behind. I watched her body how it moved against mine. I looked down taking time to admire her from feet to head. Her toes started to curling over and at that moment I knew she was about to come. I grabbed her hair wrapped it around my fingers and pulled, she threw her head back crying out more moans trying to control her breathing. I kept stroking hitting the right places to make her blow and then with a thrust from my hips and a twirl around her nipple, she climaxed. She pulled away and curled into a ball as the feeling was too great. I climbed on the bed and held her helping her control the electric orgasm.